Contents

Part Three

Part Four

Part One

Dad with Bucket and Spade

The flames are turning green.
It's a sign.

There was a time
when you could read fire.

There was a place like this
with a box of sticks in every room,

coal buckets
kept perpetually full;

scenes and shades
that blaze through,

like the thrall of a seaside train
suddenly arriving.

Grainger Market

(i)
The colour scheme of remembering:
those white geese who lost their heads,
their necks paralysed by sudden loss of thought,
their bodies cold as snowmen.

Meat hooks, claws, rabbits hung by paws,
second-hand book stalls, hams and eggs,
red-feathered hens, leather smells,
and cold damp hands, wiped pink.

Empty pigs beside trotters and snouts
that once were theirs. Butchers' fingers
in silver mincers, stained cleavers
on worn wooden blocks. Candles,

Dolly Mixtures, spiked brushes
propped outside hardware shops.
Women in headscarves laden with greens,
a juggle of juicy Jaffas.

Orange nylon nighties fluttering
from awnings, golden slippers
with cream fleece linings
and dark thick-soled socks.

(ii)
We patrol the walls of Elswick
like guards of the ancient city
waiting to greet her bus.

Greedy for what she might have
we attack the fat Saturday bags
as soon as she alights.

(iii)
She has been round all the stalls
in the thick expanding clatter
under that glittering glass,
tiptoeing sawdust, sidestepping clots,

weaving from the record shop
to Oliver's and Dodd's, past greeting cards,
the Penny Bazaar, Northern Opticals,
the flower stands and the Weigh House.

Through endless rows of fruit and veg
to rest her heavy bags and legs
by the plastic grass beside the caf'
before one last stop at Farnons

where she buys all our vests,
where you can get anything in white:
Communion dresses, pillows, sheets and nets,
all you need to keep body and soul intact.

Except those magic colouring books
she sometimes brings us back:
their grocery of greens,
barrows of reds;

just add water,
see the colours spread.

Two Easter Eggs
and a Good Clagging

I creep back as mousily as I can
both brick-thick Dairy Milk eggs
steadied against the glass door.

But Mam is already there
waiting on the other side,
wavy, yet plainly mad,

now suddenly clear
about the missing quid
and where it went.

And because of their size
there's no hiding
or denying it

and the way she's carrying on
there seems no point
in drawing attention to the fact

that only one is meant for me,
the other, a gift for my sister,
is an act of generosity.

.

The Escaped Bull

Honest Angela, it got loose,
was on the news, it's huge,
two men trampled under its hooves
as it took off like a bullet
for Scotswood.
It was last seen heading for us:
up Gloucester Street to Elswick,
its massive horns draped in guts,
dripping blood.
Yes Angela, human blood.

Do you think it can smell *us*,
you Angela, streaming snots,
that cut where we dunched heads
wet as a bowl of jelly?
Their noses are acute Angela
and they *do* like blood,
anything red in fact.
That scarlet ribbon in your plait
would be very attracting to bulls.

No Angela, don't tell your Mam.
Don't go in Angela.
Here, we'll play skipping.
Angela, I was just kidding.
They only eat boys Angela.
They don't like girls. Honest.

Momentary Fire

We wait for ages for the smoke,
confirmation of a new pope.

All that time spent, watching,
glued to the screen,

nothing happening.

Suddenly, thanks to Mam's devotion
and a Prince Brothers' promotion

we don't need Little Pauline to invite us in,
now we have our own 21" Ferguson

to see the Vatican's cross keys and crown
pass to the head of the new pope, John.

Now life can begin.
Our new religion:

the white dot on the screen
at the close of the day

fading away
at the speed of numbness.

Holy Communion Breakfast

I am holy now in veil and long white satin
dotted with moist ginger crumbs,
a stain of lime pop on my holy tongue.
The green tash my best friend is laughing at
I rise above, am holier than that, holier now than a nun.
And my best friend no longer needs to be a girl.
I am holy like a saint, like ancient Northumberland.

By the dunes on Amble seafront
our caravan awaits us. I crave long words,
drag explanations from my complicated parents.
Is a hundred pounds enough to buy a real house,
or a lifetime's supply of shop-bought miracles?
Pound upon pound I will keep for myself:
sweet seedless grapes to be blessed, tongued, squashed.
.

Little Mothers of Amble

In the next caravan three girls
in pink and white stripes, sisters
identically styled and wrapped.
You make friends of them,
the middle one especially,
whose age matches your own.
Though you admire the oldest
clever one, and the youngest
who, for the whole week,
you will make a doll of.

Playing skips and dressy-ups
you form a picture of your future self:
there you are with three daughters
all caught smiling in new red shoes.

.

Blue-bottles

On our wall they take time out
from flight and shite and buzzing.
On eyelash legs they glint
like drops of petrol.
Titchy and quick they dart in the sun.
I aim, take a run, squash them under
the ribbed soles of my fresh white sandals.
Summer's death toll caked in. Numbing.
I skip home for Sunday dinner. Humming.

.

Child with Fever

The empty grate
in the big cold bedroom,
filled with light.
The snap of sticks,
coal fragments jumping out
onto the tiled hearth.
The scrunch of buckets,
patter of sparks,
silky licks of flame
rainbowing the dark.

Your limp hands raised to the wall,
your head, strange as an octopus.
The whole room charged
by your sickness:
parents who will fetch and carry
until the day your colour returns,
when the grate gets brushed,
the ashes removed, the hearth wiped,
the mantle-shelf dusted again to clean black marble.
When the crooked finger of school beckons you back.
.

Dad with Cigarette

The put, put, put of his wet mouth
encircling the filter. His bronchial cough,
chuckled spit: a hanging green bulb
of phlegm drying out above the fire.

From behind his *Daily Mirror*
a long slow exhale,
a stream-lined trail of smoke,
crackle and wheeze of pleasure.

I tap the poker on the crisping snot,
try to drop it from my line of vision
but his eagle ears are all a glisten.

Divvin't ye knock that off, he says.
Divvin't touch it. It's lucky.

Sisterhood

She said: If I ever took
another pair of her socks,
if she ever caught me
in another pair of her socks,
ever, ever again,
she would hack my feet off
and my heart out.

A joke, I felt
but it's two hours since
I locked myself in here
after she appeared from nowhere
slicing the air at my ankles
with a cleaver, and I cleared
sixteen stairs like an Olympic star.

It's two hours
since the rutting commenced
on the other side of this door;
her snorting like a demented cow,
shining her blade
through the keyhole,
and one mad, green eye.

Mission Box

When the Brothers of St Vincent de Paul
call in to relieve it,
we watch them peel the seal
tip the contents from the secret door
onto the spread out *Chronicle*,
then count it, put it in to a black bag
and exit. Easy as that.

And to think of all the trouble I have
just nabbing enough for ten tabs
and a bag of Harrogate toffee.
Slicing at the up-side-down slot,
risking my wrists with the sharpest knife,
arms above my head like lumps of lead.
Trying to glide my blade past the copper

guide out the silver.

Six Foot End
for Anne Clewes

I see her face
as I surface
for the last time.

She has red eyes
leaking black chlorine liner
down her white cheeks.

She has a life-saver
certificate
and big floater tits

flattened now
against her blue
ribbon-bedecked swimsuit.

We are blood sisters,
have the scars
and identical tattoos.

I have no more breath,
have bobbed up
for one last look.

I see her face:
the only one to move
forward from the line,

her lovely face
as I surface
for the last time.

The Day I Was Strangled

We sit on wooden desks
that stink of sour milk.
Round my neck
the blue and gold striped
invitation of a new school scarf.

This lunch time semi-circle
fading in and out
as a carrot-topped nutter
I never met in my life
beds me into the new hierarchy.

Woodland Path to the Asylum
after Van Gogh

My short frilled socks
are wet on my ankles.
I am trying not to panic

as birdsong retreats
and silence grows under
the heavy weight of thorn.

I want the sun to reappear, chase
these black leaves and twigs,
the jagged sticks that gash my legs.

If you could please throw down
a path, a pink path that leads
back to our egg-yolk-house

where I imagine ourselves
with catalogues, cutting out
pictures, inventing lives:

handsome, well-heeled families
whose biggest cause of worry
is how to harness the horse.

After the Dance

The boy had watched her
heel and toe, heel and toe.
She had cement feet and claggy hands
and arms that flapped like crows.

She puts on another lump of coal,
wipes her hand on her Ma's overall,
imagines herself pretty, him smiling
back, at the mirror-propped wall.

But there is a smudge of soot.
How long has it been there?
Did he see, or care?
Did he notice it beneath her hair?

Him in real leather
Cuban-heeled boots.
Him, with the soft fringe,
and the sweet dream looks.

She feels thick and blunt
like a flat-headed hammer.
She takes the poker
and turns it over, again and again.

Birthday Treat

In my purple, mini, drummer-boy coat
and slinky white, knee-length boots
I come towards you in the snow,
your black overcoat
sugared like a Rowntree's Fruit Pastel.

Sestina on Knees

At the onset of the cold season
old people drop to their knees,
praise and plead in the church of the Beatitudes.
You are black and blue
from hope, stained-glass winter sun, and visions
of saints rippling on baptismal water.

The one you dream of: unfathomed waters.
Your youth, with all the brevity of the season's
fashion: platform boots that kill your knees,
two bone china cups of purity,
your mouth clattering blue,
in the purple, drummer-boy coat. A mini vision

freezing at the park stop, where a bus comes into view,
throwing up sludge and sleet and water
on a whirl of winter passengers, this unseasonal
weather on the queue of knocking knees,
all their stiff garments, late November blessing.
Their collective thanks and curses raised to the blue.

On board the steam-clad bus, the air is thick, blue:
they've *waited over a fuckin hour* for this vision.
Public transport systems make their eyes water.
The Corporation's bus fleet in the snowy season
is as useless a dead men's knees;
deaf to workers needs, petitions, blessings.

Now in the church of the Beatitudes
the early risers pock-marked blue
represent unsightly visions,
their sleep washed out in sinks of ice-water.
Their flasks of tea and wax-wrapped bait, seasoned
to perfection, wait, fresh as freed-up knees

which after Mass, quickly go in peace. First-Friday-knees
hurry to bus queues, the Shipyard Beatitudes:
pay day for Boiler Suits, every shade and shape of blue.
You think of the apprentice boy holding a vision,
the day he prays for, when spring waters
melt away this sexless season.

Seasoned in spring fires, all his desire stirred, his needs
beatified, he will glide out of the blue,
a vision from the future: he and you, merging
                                    like warm water.

Age of Innocence

The man with the Hungarian tie
wants to pay you in
to a Hammer Horror classic
at the Rex.

He wants to bite your nails
trail your hand across his crotch,
draw back the screen
deliver the shock,

confirm what he suspects:
your mouth stretched
in the darkness,
all ignorance and startlement.

Biology

In the front seat
last week
he said I was
green as grass.

Tonight on the couch
I put my head
on his lap.

(He has a car,
his own flat,
and stacks of money.)

He places an open book
on me.
This page explores
female anatomy.

Part Two

Notes Towards a Change of Season

Tracks a car left in the snow.
A milk float.
Three blackbirds soft as dust.

Lesson

In the black of night they curl
in the dunes and wait,
sunrise brings low tide
and still dark pools,

a chance to slip out of their clothes
observe themselves in the collected water.
They are white ash
and have feet like plums.

Swaddling

Why does the sky start
catching at my ankles like surf?

Down off those tiptoes, cheats.
You can't all be that tall.

It throws me back.
Those small bundles I wrapped,

curly fingers,
the shape of them in cotton sheets.

That shade of pink makes me think
of something I can't think of.

My mouth salivating colours,
rainbows and sweet wrappers,

Quality Street, Roses:
ladies twirled for the ball.

Musicianship

You are all standing inside a big egg
under my dress, under my skin,

a collective of daughters
tapping the curves of my violin.

I feel you nestle me under your chin,
your eager limbs rippling silk.

You are tweaking my strings,
making notes, practicing skills:

the music to come,
the thrills.

Slaughtered

They all crowd in.
Someone who can't bear to look
crouches under the bed.
Once you're out
they wash you, weigh you,
put you in a plastic basket and leave.

Only me left with two old sows
who grunt over my carcass,
clean between my legs,
knuckle soap into my armpits
while they talk about going to market,
the abbatoir, the exorbitant price of pig.

For the next nine weeks
I believe my head
has slipped off my neck,
but I must make the effort,
must smarten myself,
straighten my aching back.

My split pubic bone will reconnect.
I will put on the white dress,
the red beads, some earrings, a belt.
I will pad out against spilt blood,
entrust you to someone else
for the first time.

REM

I am taking a taxi to a Turkish market,
to a stall that sells stones like pink teeth.

The bazaar's antidote to all complaints:
cure-alls I swallow like aspirins.

Dream pills. Sweet dreams.
Some say they don't, but

see her feet running the fells,
her knees bent in prayer,

her toes squeezing lemons,
her hands skimming the keys of a baby grand.

See her lips singing jazz,
her eyebrows solving the case of the missing sugar,

her tongue sweet with the taste of its sudden return.

Childsight

for Sarah

The things you teach me:
the meaning of the word organic,
the behaviour of a jar of maggots,
subjects of power and authority.

I lean on a tree, strain to hear
the earth's message.
You say: Shadow is a place
the sun can't see.

Asthmatic

Tomorrow my love
I will powder your cheeks with blusher,
pat your lips with colour,
cover the rings under your eyes, and beam.

I will tighten the belt on your loose skirt,
tuck in your baggy school shirt,
carry your heavy bag, then wave you off,
inhaler in pocket

and an Excuse Me note for Miss Potts:
Please excuse Rachael for staying off.
If she vomits today don't worry,
she does this a lot.

Then I will trade the city dust
for sand and salt sea.
Me, breathing in healthy air,
guilty in the first degree.

Argument

She says nothing,

so I say: love,
or should say love

but instead I say:
Have some fucking sense,
don't take a job in a nightclub.

And she says: I'll see you
at Christmas then.

And I say: All mothers
should be stood up against a wall
and shot. Come home,

come home and watch me drink
this rum, this whiskey.

And she says: Do what you like,
but don't touch my ouzo, will you.

Reflections from a Train Window
for Leah

A waistcoat she had suddenly arriving in my head,
gold, green and red, double-breasted,
spilled on the couch like forgotten wine,
claggy hands, cardigans, County Girl tights.

Houses, thin and fat, names that write themselves
on the glass: York, Darlington, Durham.

Storm clouds like squirrels,
smuts of rain waiting to fall, held up like love
until the weight of it all
pours down on her small golden head.

Turbulence

Travelling.
The illusion of being still.

Sun on a lake
swamped in petrol.

Tarquin serving in Borders.
A drugs drop on Essex Road,

police in purple latex gloves
searching suspects at a bus stop.

Colours clashing: business-blue
on real-estate-red.

Offices, mountains of latticework,
and clouds like brains.

I am clearing my head
with lemon cake in John Lewis

as Sarah strides through
Oxford Street with purpose.

River Tyne Refinement

In daylight the Sage Music Centre looks like those old rain hats
our mams concertinaed out over wash-and-sets,
tidy as the new waterfront: its green glass mirroring
a taxi cab, a metallic cyclist buzzing past,
his stiff blue-bottle toes, his sun-glass eyes: *The Fly.*

Walking by, an identikit couple in dark suits and white ties
listen to birdsong, the river, vibrations from the Millennium Bridge,
where a man with both arms bandaged from elbow to wrist
smiles in the wind, tries to light his tab.

Women sailing on *The Island Scene* flash waxed legs and chiffon frills,
command the Swing Bridge to open, and it does.
Silk scarves flutter on their scented necks, where a pack of midges drill.

At the Copthorne Hotel they turn and clink, bunting waves
to the shoremen in deck chairs fishing under the Metro Bridge,
their Toon tops branded with early evening shadow.

My phone goes. Rachael wants to know how to bake a potato.
I listen to the summer sun, think, try to remember the regulo;
the sound of my own voice echoes over the Quay, up to the Keep.

Lost gauges of heat, customs and speech, lying deep in the river.

War, Baby

She is running out of adolescence,
is planning trips to Rome and Venice,
Thailand and Madrid.

But the edge of her spade is sharp
and itches for one last dig
in the loft of his sick toys:

their necks drawn with dotted lines
as if decapitation were welcome
and *Cut Here* the development
of a brainchild;

as if there was no such thing
as emotional intelligence,
or space, or distance.
The only truth in existence:

revenge.

Meat Substitute
for Rachael

Your poor pale blue veins,
run down slip of a girl.

Here, try this map out:
this new geography.

Let's get vitamins into you,
enliven the head and the blood.

Let's pack him off
bring you back to your heart.

Dexterity

Your mobile matches the tight lime jumper
you just bought from H&M.

I pour myself tea and relax
while you drink, eat and text.

Your thumb has become steroid thick,
is loud, and quick as a moped.

The lad on the next bench
looks like that TV ad's Benefit Cheat.

He sneaks a hand into his jacket,
brings out a trembling phone.

It is mooing like a cow.
He speaks to it to calm it down.

Tardis to Puerto del Carmen

In the Doctor's driving mirror I see
lines come and go around my mouth.

From the rear seat three smart young women
reflect back an image of my children.

They talk about the perfect orange moon
as my head turns into an egg and disappears.

Talk Later

It's snowing.

A collared dove
is nesting here.

Three blackbirds are whistling.

Thank you for the lovely
butterfly book.

Cheers for the theatre treat.
Home sweet home.

Luv u.

Luv u 2.

Wish we could write.

John Bull
from Dog Leap Stairs

On the quay a wooden clog,
a snake, and a shell, wriggle
themselves into the water.

The pubs and hotels are lifting
as England go two: nil up.

In Offshore Bar a hairless ape
intimidates the girls,

offers them a kiss on his bald pate,
on the painted cross of St. George.

Later I dream of him unclothed,
in he goes, wrapped in a flag,
with a stone, and a rope.

Sensuous

Daughters, smell this green silk cape,
taste this raspberry satin,
feel this quilt
padded with the pattern of a spring garden.

See the curve of these lace ribbons,
hear that crepe crackle - yellow!
Girls, these fellows don't know
the meaning of the word.

Part Three

Primitive

The smell of herring
smoking.

A joint of wood
crackling out its final secrets,

being in this moment

both wood and fire,
lake and fish.

Lake on April 1st

Small shift
from earth to stars.
The short time
before it all dissolves.
Stars we gaze up to,
patterns we read,
move and remove.
A practical joke:
here today, and gone.
The lake tonight
covered by a full moon.
I could raise my arms,
skate on its sleek white skin.

The Lost Art of Making Fire

The first whoosh of paper.
The excitement and the danger.

You forget how much tending
it takes. The coaxing of the black

into smoke. Then out of the blue
green flame, yellow fire.

Wind in the grate
irrespective of the weather.

Firewall

I get into bed with the last
leaps of fire plastering the wall.

Sometimes things squeeze through:
these full-bloomed nasturtiums

lovingly restored,
papering the room with dance.

The Night of the Hunted

Blue smoke nervously
broaching the chimney,
your fur like a soft brush
swept across
your sucked out brain.

You are deluded, not hidden.
Your head sticking out
like a moose on a plaque,
eyes too far apart
for the confines of the room.

You should be out in the wild,
your antlers rattling,
instead of under a clock,
stuck fast, inhaling, afraid
of setting off the alarm.

Blue smoke nervously
broaches the chimney,
your fur like a soft brush
sweeps across
your sucked out brain.

Mr Clean

He sits there in the afternoon air
of the cosy kitchen, recollecting
all kinds of calumny against him.

In general, he thinks our society
is far too accommodating.
This thinking pleases him
as he sips further
on his green organic tea.

Refreshed and rising to his subject
he proceeds to make a mental list:
all the things that tolerant people,
like himself, should no longer tolerate.

He puts Drunks at the top,
then Smoking, then Drugs.
He pauses to tongue
a hunk of freshly slaughtered beast.

The animal was a prize bull.

He is stirred,
inclining to his full weight.

Himself and bull
inseparate.

The Enemy

They came across the border
painted blue back then,
noses sliced, clamours screaming.

You knew where you were:
a vixen was a vicious vixen,
a sheep was a simple sheep,
not smiles and deceit,
cheese-teeth and flattery.

See this flea-ridden fleece:
the grin, as if it can't wait to be
your best Sunday coat.

And Some will be Called Janet
And Some will be Called Johnny

There's a fly on your eyelid.
It has a face like a spool.
It talks to the four winds:
incessant, never stopping for breath
or interruption.

It has a collection of marshmallow foam
in the corner of its mouth.
Its words go in and out,
congealed and sticky,
spreading over you like mouldy jam.

More flies come,
their obsequious tongues
slobbering on:
their fur hats and hidden microphones.

This one has an Edinburgh accent,
that spits out slaver and crumbs,
that sucks out your tear ducts
and every expression but horror.

Fire at Midnight

If you rearrange the sticks
you can resurrect the flame,

tired though it is
it will rise up again.

One last effort will bring
the colour to your cheeks.

See.

You are blushing:
the heat is coming back.

With a little prodding
your blood remembers everything.

Fire Myth

The first time we made love
was late one Saturday
on the floor by the fire.
It was planned out,
no light, only an apricot glow
flickering on the mat.

We were actors
in a grand romance.
We glowed peach,
our limbs licked,
blazing fruit from coal.

But it was early yet, still spring,
and there was always something
in this place:
creaks and aches,
groans and mutterings.

The dead servants
on the top floor,
their sexless frippery rustling,
a howling gale
blowing under the door.

Little Death by Fire

It's hard not to
have an asthma attack
having sex on the mat,
with your head
bashing off the poker,
and your shoulder
pounding off the hearth,
stirring cat fur and ash,
black spelks
that lodge in your back,
set your teeth rictus
like disco dentures.
And it's so white
and so cold,
late snow on the sills
piling like dandruff
under violet rays.

Company of Fire

We progressed away from it
to the electric bar,
learned of elements,
false flames that lick
cold eggs of gas;
patterns that recreate themselves
over and over: imitations,
identikit.

So that in old age
all you have for comfort
is a cigarette,
no paper, or sticks,
no coal, or logs:
a switch, a Superking, a match,
nothing else
to intercept the loneliness.

Eventual

in memory of Teresa Kenny

If you wait long enough
the candle will put itself out,
and the fire too;
the chatter will die,
and the lamp's comfort.

See now, hush:
the choking flames
gyrating,
the last seconds
before they give up.

Arms in splints
to stop them waving,
to prevent them wrenching out
the futile feeding tube,
ease such irritation.

Be patient.
If you wait long enough
they will let you go out.
Silence will erupt:
the dark will overcome.

Banshee

Two candles gleam on the table.
You await his signal
to squeeze the life from them.

The flames glitter
on your frail neck,
a watery white

that might be sliced
with one quick slip
of a blade.

The last dying log is turned
in the grate, it is shaped like a face.
You fancy you can hear it scream.

Tab Ends

When they find them in the ashes
as they rake tomorrow's coals

I will deny any knowledge:
my ten passports,

all those trips to Thailand
and the Middle East.

Their security
is not what it's cracked up to be:

mug shots, searches,
customs, duties, lies.

*

Oh for the reign
of street tab machines

when cigarette cases
were not the only places

to explain
death and disease;

when all we terrorists
had to effect

was how to supply
with foreign coins

each other's cigarettes.

Smokers' Echo

Necks stretched like swans
we slide down the world.

Race Week thrill, rides
as polished as banisters.

We curve through the fair,
hot fumes swirling,

the cheers of our fellows
juddering over the Moor.

Smoke curling everywhere,
blue rings and laughter.

We are all revellers.
This is the life!

The Morning After

The inside of my head
like devasted loins
after birth.

Ploughed fields
to be healed,
reset by spring.

Above us
five white clouds
and blue sky.

Preserve in Oils

Let's take some time out,
have a bite in this caf'
we will paint into our memories.

It will occupy a small space,
a tiny canvas,
yellow walls and green shutters.

But the shutters will be open.
We will keep them open
always.

Between these two colours
we will have a burst of flowers,
pink and white, picked out:

permanently in bloom,
full bloom,
standing out from everything.

Part Four

Marginalia

You made Regret cocktails,
painted your nails Regret pink,
slipped back into the margins
where you found a place
to animate

this gander, full of himself.
No trace of who he was,
his name, or species,
what he did,
or what he meant to you.

This careful study. (Yours.)

AM

Connecting her stilettos
with the concrete path
she feels light as a paper hat.

From the house opposite
someone waves
from an open sash.

He has a bare chest
and a brown hat
and a slice of sun lighting him.

A new day seeps
into her linen dress,
the silver mesh,

their thin summer.

Eve Realises Her Purpose
then Becomes Catholic

Adam's head lifts
as she sits straddled above him.

The pain in his side is her fault,
they both know this

but there is something about
what she does

that makes up for the loss,
the damage.

Tomorrow they will learn

how to chicken farm,
how to scratch out a living.

They will learn all about
the behaviour of the barnyard:

the big red hen of guilt,
the small red cock of pleasure.

Smitten

You have on your recital shirt,
your sonneteering waistcoat.
Our cigarettes kiss
as your fists jut like knuckle-dusters
over my thumbs.
In the Ted Hughes' Wine Bar
I gift you
a chunk-chain necklace
from the Diamond Shop,
present it
over a red-check table cloth
as the waiter leans across
to light the candle
between our fire.

**The Symbols of Love
are Everywhere**

There is a red rose above each of us,
two red roses big as sun hats,
big as tiger-flaps,
big as villas.

There are no blue monsters
unless you open the door.

Aurora Borealis
in Exhibition Park

In a pink haze of children
we are playing on the slides.

Circling the boating lake,
we are in each other's eyes,

preparing to make
an exhibition of ourselves.

Re-Creation

How long is it since we felt like this?

Doing roly-polies, summersaults,
standing on our heads,
rolling in the grass.

There is gold, yellow, lemon, sunshine.
Then there is sunshine, lemon, yellow, gold.

Look at us tumbling about.

Our hair is in knots.
We are climbing the forbidden rocks.

No one is hurt.
No one is fallen.

The Parkie's in his house,
he's not coming out,
nothing can spoil it.

The Song of the Decorator

At the top of the ladder you paint
yet another room magnolia.

This lack of colour has you glum.

Tonight I will take the turpentine
to you, will rub you clean.

We will drink purple rum,
eat blue cheese,

glow like green Spangles:
the best flavour ever.

Amorphous
Chagall Museum, Nice

Someone is praying
at the mosaic wall,
rubbing his forehead
as if it were sweating gold.

For a second I see
you crossing the compass,
our skin and muscle
fused, melded.

Chagall said everything
is possible
if it is based upon love.

And in this one beat
of searing will
you are with me here
drinking all of this in.

Premonition

You hold your cigarette
like a dart,
while my ankles are crossed
like swords.

Sunlight frames the wall,
showing up the cracks
in the green plaster.

Let's stretch for it,
try and catch some warmth
before it goes.

In the Drink

Under the sea
your reptile wings are useless.

Knives of water are sharpening,

sharks of glass are massing,
heading our way.

Coitus Non Starter

You are lying on a rock
blind drunk. Should I finish
the other half of this bottle
or pour it over your head?

I'd imagined sex,
getting lost
in our own private heaven.
But your legs are stuck,

you are dreaming of your other love
who is nagging over us,
warning you not to give her up:
sobrietous folly.

Your eyelids are marching off,
you are receptive to her voice,
its seductive slosh
warming your innards.

Writing with Gloves on

You leave, but still
I let you back

to grind more ash,
to fall in the bath:

your wrecking spree,
your last laugh, your thievery.

In real time, here at the shore
the tide goes out, and in.

A stranger leans down, slowly
performs a cleansing ritual

I am drawn to follow.

Night Time with Socks

I lock up, count
the smoked cigarettes:
ten mine, none yours.
I curl up
on my own side
try not to think
about your hair,
or mouth,
but of how
I will thaw out
eventually,
even with your side empty.

Analysand

The sky like wrapping paper,
and a dress she used to wear:
a tent dress, psychedelic,
violet swirls and targets,
turquoise bulls-eyes

where it would hurt
to be shot,
but off from the arteries
and vital organs;

so that, with her bold helmet
and socks, and her shield
designed to conceal blood
no one would ever need to guess
anything, except that she survived.

All Saints

These smashed lids lifted free. The earth beneath:
a testimony of Coke cans and broken bottles strewn like flowers.

Always wild up here:
the slatted fence, its wires twisting off into the ravine of rabbits.

Those who died, the overgrown, the broken, these stone monuments
chipping free, disintegrating with bark and twigs and nettles.

Sillicks' grave tilts like a boat,
is gnarled with love: Here is the burial place of all the above.

There is a rainbow coming up over the Sage,
its humps rising with church bells and garlic smells to meet it.

There are cranes overhead and green hair nets on half built blocks.
From this hill, arches and roof tops.

The Tyne Bridge, Pilgrim Street, cut across by motorway.
The Pilgrim's Way you can no longer follow.

Past and present living it up. Bar 55 in its pink flourescence.
A lump of new houses on the ancient path.

Damp auld trees that hang about the arse end of the graveyard and snigger,
whisper about the lairds of the past, the scaffolds of the future.

The cladding that comes to pass.
Live Theatre, bistros, and always the river.

Acknowledgements

With thanks to the editors of the following poetry magazines
in which versions of some of these poems have appeared:
*Global Tapestry, Iota, The Linkway, Never Bury Poetry,
The New Writer, The North, Orbis, Other Poetry, Pennine
Platform, Pulsar, Rain Dog, Reach, Staple, Quantum Leap.*

'Sensuous' was a winner of the Amnesty postcard competition
for International Women's Day. 'Dad with Cigarette' was
commissioned by the Sammy Johnson Memorial Trust.
'Escaped Bull' and 'Sisterhood' were first published in
Bliddy Tales: an anthology.

I am indebted as always to everyone who supports me in my
writing. In compiling this collection particular appreciation
goes to Ally May and Kevin Cadwallender, and to the Tyrone
Guthrie Centre at Annaghmakerrig where some of these
poems were begun.